Top 30 Mos~~t~~ Ribs Recipes

A Ribs Cookbook with Pork, Beef and Lamb

by Graham Bourdain

Copyright © 2017 Graham Bourdain

All Rights Reserved

This book contains material protected under International and Federal Copyright Laws and Treaties. Any unauthorized reprint or use of this material is prohibited. No part of this book may be reproduced or transmitted in any form or by any means, electronic or mechanical, including photocopying, recording, or by any information storage and retrieval system without express written permission from the author.

Disclaimer

Reasonable care has been taken to ensure that the information presented in this book is accurate. However, the reader should understand that the information provided does not constitute legal, medical or professional advice of any kind.

No Liability: this product is supplied "as is" and without warranties. All warranties, express or implied, are hereby disclaimed. Use of this product constitutes acceptance of the "No Liability" policy. If you do not agree with this policy, you are not permitted to use or distribute this product.

We shall not be liable for any losses or damages whatsoever (including, without limitation, consequential loss or damage) directly or indirectly arising from the use of this product.

Table of Contents

1. Oven-Baked Barbecue Baby Back Ribs 6

2. Oven-Baked Garlic Prime Rib 8

3. Grilled Korean Barbecue Short Ribs 10

4. Grilled Maple Glazed Ribs 12

5. Slow Cooker Back Ribs 14

6. Grilled Whisky Baby Back Ribs 16

7. Oven-Baked Worcestershire Spareribs 18

8. Baby Bite Sweet n' Sour Pork Ribs 20

9. Oven-Baked Sherry Braised Short Ribs 22

10. Oven-Baked Honey Garlic Ribs 24

11. Oven-Baked Kiwi-Lime Pork Ribs 26

12. Grilled Cranberry Glazed Pork Ribs 28

13. Oven-Baked Chinese Spareribs 30

14. Grilled St. Louis-style Spareribs 32

15. Grilled Coconut Spareribs 34

16. Oven-Baked Cherry Short Ribs 36

17. Oven-Baked Plum Glazed Pork Ribs 38

18. Grilled Raspberry Chipotle Back Ribs 40

19. Oven-Baked Hoisin Ribs 42

20. Oven-Baked Cabernet Beef Short Ribs 44

21. Grilled Tennessee Style Back Ribs 46

22. Oven-Baked Asian Back Ribs 48

23. Grilled Sticky Molasses Spareribs 50

24. Grilled Peach Glazed Ribs 52

25. Grilled Kansas Barbecued Spareribs 54

26. Grilled Missouri Style St. Louis Ribs 56

27. Grilled Cider Spareribs 58

28. Grilled Lemon Pepper Pork Back Ribs 60

29. Oven-Baked Hawaiian Spareribs 62

30. Sesame and Root Beer Glazed Ribs 64

1. Oven-Baked Barbecue Baby Back Ribs

Prep: 15 min. Cook: 2h 50 min. Ready in: 3h 20 min. Servings: 4

Ingredients:

½ cup ancho chili powder
¼ cup brown sugar
¼ cup white sugar
¼ cup salt
2 tbsp. freshly ground black pepper
1 tbsp. ground cumin
1 tsp. dry mustard
1 tsp. ground cayenne pepper
½ tsp. ground dried chipotle pepper
1 rack baby back pork ribs
1 cup barbecue sauce

Cooking Directions:

Start by preheating your oven to 250 degrees F (120 degrees C).
Then you mix the ancho chili powder, brown sugar, white sugar, salt, black pepper, cumin, dry mustard, cayenne pepper and chipotle pepper in a bowl until thoroughly mixed.
Then place the ribs meat-side down on aluminum foil. Use a knife to prick the back of the rib rack several times and generously apply the seasoning mix to all sides of the rib rack.
With the rib rack meat-side down, wrap foil around it to create a good seal and transfer the meat to a sheet pan.
Bake in the preheated oven until tender and cooked, about 2 hours. Take the meat out and let it cool for 15 minutes.
Increase the oven temperature to 350 degrees F (175 degrees C). Unwrap the meat and drain the juices and fat, then brush barbecue sauce on all sides of the rib rack.
Place the rib rack meat-side up and return to oven, leaving the foil open. Bake for 10 minutes and then brush another layer of barbeque sauce on meat-side only. Repeat baking and brushing with sauce 3 more times, for a total of 40 minutes baking time.
Cut the rib rack into individual ribs and serve with more barbecue sauce.

Enjoy

2. Oven-Baked Garlic Prime Rib

Prep: 10 min. Cook: 1h 30 min. Ready in: 1h 40 min. Servings: 15

Ingredients:

1 (10 pound) prime rib roast

10 cloves of minced garlic

2 tbsp. olive oil

2 tsp. salt

2 tsp. ground black pepper

2 tsp. dried thyme

Cooking Directions:

Start by placing the rib roast in a roasting pan fatty side up. Thoroughly mix together the minced garlic, olive oil, salt, pepper and thyme. Spread the mix over the roast and let the roast sit until it is at room temperature. No more than 1 hour.

Preheat the oven to 500 degrees F (260 degrees C).

Roast the rib roast for 20 min. in the preheated oven. Reduce temperature to 325 degrees F (165 degrees C), and continue roasting for another 60 – 75 min. The internal temperature of the roast should be at 135 degrees F (57 degrees C) for medium rare.

Let the roast rest for 10 – 15 min. before carving the meat, so it can retain its juices.

Enjoy

3. Grilled Korean Barbecue Short Ribs

Prep: 15 min. Cook: 10 min. Ready in: 7 h 25 min. Servings: 5

Ingredients:
¾ cup water
¾ cup soy sauce
3 tbsp. white vinegar
¼ cup dark brown sugar
2 tbsp. white sugar
1 tbsp. black pepper
2 tbsp. sesame oil
¼ cup minced garlic
½ large, minced onion
3 pounds of Korean-style short ribs

Cooking Directions:

Start by pouring water, soy sauce and vinegar into a non-metallic bowl. Then add in the brown sugar, white sugar, pepper, sesame oil, garlic and onion. Whisk the mixture until the sugars have dissolved. Put the ribs in the newly made marinade and cover with plastic wrap. Refrigerate between 7 to 12 hours – the longer, the better for the marinade to really work.
Preheat an outdoor grill till medium-high heat.
Take the ribs out of the marinade and give them a gentle shake to remove excess marinade.
Cook on the preheated grill until the ribs are no longer pink (approx. 5-7 minutes per side).

Enjoy

4. Grilled Maple Glazed Ribs

Prep: 10 min. Cook: 1h 25 min. Ready in: 3h 40 min. Servings: 6

Ingredients:

3 pounds baby back pork ribs
¾ cup maple syrup
2 tbsp. brown sugar
2 tbsp. ketchup
1 tbsp. cider vinegar
1 tbsp. Worcestershire sauce
½ tsp. salt
½ tsp. mustard powder

Cooking Directions:

Start by placing the ribs in a pot and cover them with water. Let the ribs simmer for 1 hour or until the meat is tender. Drain the water and put the ribs on a dish.

Take a small saucepan and mix maple syrup, brown sugar, ketchup, vinegar, Worcestershire sauce, salt and mustard powder.

Bring the marinade to a low boil and cook for approx. 5 min, while stirring frequently. Let the marinade cool a little and then pour it over the ribs. Let the ribs marinate in the refrigerator for 2 hours.

Prepare the grill for cooking with indirect heat.

Remove the ribs from the marinade and pour the marinade in a saucepan and bring it to a low boil. Oil your grilling grate before transferring ribs and let the ribs cook for approx. 20 min. Baste with the marinade frequently until the ribs have a nice glaze.

__Enjoy__

5. Slow Cooker Back Ribs

Prep: 10 min. Cook: 4h 10 min. Ready in: 4h 20 min. Servings: 6

Ingredients:

3 pound baby back ribs
To taste salt
To taste pepper
½ cup water
½ sliced onion
1 clove minced garlic
1 bottle barbecue sauce

Cooking Directions:

Start by seasoning the ribs with the salt and pepper. Pour water into the slow cooker. Stack the ribs in the slow cooker and top it off with onion and garlic.

Either cook on High for 4 hours or on Low for 8 hours. Preheat the oven to 375 degrees F (190 degrees C).

Put the ribs on a sheet pan and coat the ribs with barbecue sauce. Bake the ribs in the oven until the barbecue sauce caramelizes and sticks to the meat (approx. 10 – 15 minutes)

<u>Enjoy</u>

6. Grilled Whisky Baby Back Ribs

Prep: 20 min. Cook: 2h 40 min. Ready in: 3h Servings: 4

Ingredients:

2 (2 pound) baby back pork rib racks
coarsely ground black pepper
1 tbsp. ground red chili pepper
2 ¼ tbsp. vegetable oil
½ cup minced onion
1 ½ cups water
½ cup tomato paste
½ cup white vinegar
½ brown sugar
2 ½ tbsp. honey
2 tbsp. Worcestershire sauce
2 tsp. salt
¼ tsp coarsely ground black pepper
1 ¼ tsp liquid smoke flavoring
2 tsp. whiskey
2 tsp. garlic powder
¼ tsp paprika
½ tsp. onion powder
1 tbsp. dark molasses
½ tbsp. ground red chili pepper

Cooking Directions:

Start by preheating your oven to 300 degrees F (150 degrees C). Then you cut each rack of ribs in half making 4 half racks. Sprinkle salt and pepper and 1 tbsp. chili pepper over the ribs. Wrap each half rack in aluminum foil. Bake for 2 ½ hours.

While they are baking, heat oil in a saucepan over medium heat. Stir onion in the oil for 5 min. Stir in the water, tomato paste, vinegar, brown sugar, honey and Worcestershire sauce. Season with 2 tsp. salt, ¼ tsp. black pepper, liquid smoke, whiskey, garlic powder, paprika, onion powder, dark molasses and ½ tbsp. ground red chili pepper. Bring the mix up to a boil and lower the heat. Let it simmer for 1 ¼ hours or until the sauce thickens.

Remove the sauce from heat and put it aside.

Now you preheat an outdoor grill to high heat. Remove the ribs from the oven and place them on the grill.

Grill the ribs for approx. 4-5 minutes on each side. Put the sauce on the ribs right before they are done grilling.

Enjoy

7. Oven-Baked Worcestershire Spareribs

Prep: 10 min. Cook: 1h Ready in: 2h Servings: 4

Ingredients:

4 pounds pork spareribs
1 ½ cups ketchup
½ cup barbecue sauce
½ cup brown sugar
1 ½ tbsp. lemon juice
1tsp. Worcestershire sauce
¼ tsp hot pepper sauce
1 ½ steak sauce
1 clove minced garlic

Cooking Directions:

Start by placing the ribs in a pot with enough water to cover. Let the water boil and cook the ribs on medium-high heat for 1 hour.
Then preheat oven to 350 degrees F (175 degrees C).
Use a saucepan to mix ketchup, barbecue sauce, brown sugar, lemon juice, Worcestershire sauce, hot pepper sauce, steak sauce and garlic. Let the sauce sit on medium high heat for approx. 20 min.
Slice the ribs between the bones place them on a sheet pan. Pour the sauce over the ribs and cover them with aluminum foil and bake for approx. 30 min. Then remove the foil and continue baking for approx. 30 min.

Enjoy

8. Baby Bite Sweet n' Sour Pork Ribs

Prep: 15 min. Cook: 1h 10 min. Ready in: 1h 25 min. Servings: 4

Ingredients:

1 cup white sugar
¼ cup flour
1 tsp. salt
½ tsp. pepper
½ tsp. dry mustard
2 cups water
½ cup soy sauce
½ cup vinegar
2 pounds pork spareribs cut into baby bites
1 tbsp. vegetable oil
2 cloves chopped garlic

Cooking Directions:

Start by taking a bowl and mix the sugar, flour, salt, pepper and mustard. Then you mix in the water, soy sauce and vinegar.
Put the ribs in a pot and cover them with water. Bring to a boil on medium-high heat and let them cook for 10 min, then drain.
Take a pan and heat the oil on medium-high heat. Brown the ribs on all sides. Now pour in the sauce and stir. Bring the ribs to a boil, reduce the heat and let them simmer for 30 min.
Add the garlic and continue simmering for approx. 15 min.

Enjoy

9. Oven-Baked Sherry Braised Short Ribs

Prep: 20 min. Cook: 2h 35 min. Ready in: 2h 55 min. Servings: 8

Ingredients:

4 slices bacon, cut into ½ inch pieces
3 ½ pounds beef short ribs
To taste salt
To taste pepper
6 sprigs of fresh thyme without leaves
1 bay leaf
1 diced onion
3 cloves minced garlic
2 tbsp. flour
1 cup dry sherry
1 liter beef broth

Cooking Directions:

Start by preheating the oven to 350 degrees F (175 degrees C).
Put the bacon in a pan and cook over medium-high heat. Flip them until evenly browned, approx. 10 min. Move the bacon to an oven-ready pot and keep the bacon fat in the pan.
Continue heating the bacon fat while seasoning the short ribs with salt and pepper. Cook the short ribs in the bacon fat until browned on all sides, approx. 4 – 5 min per side. Transfer the ribs to the oven-ready pot, while saving the bacon fat in the pan.
Reduce the heat under the pan to medium and cook the onions until golden and soft. Now add the garlic and cook until fragrant, approx. 30 sec.
Add flour into the mix and stir until the mixture becomes almost like a paste and light golden, approx. 2 – 3 min.
Add sherry into the onion mixture. Let it cook until it thickens, approx. 3 min. Pour the sherry-onion mix into the oven-ready pot and add the beef broth. Bring the ribs up to a simmer and cover the pot with a lid.
Put the oven-ready pot in the pre-heated oven and bake the short ribs for approx. 2 hours or until fork tender.
Take out the ribs and keep the sauce in the pot. Increase the oven to high heat and reduce the sauce until thickened, approx. 10 min.
Pour the sauce over the ribs and serve.

Enjoy

10. Oven-Baked Honey Garlic Ribs

Prep: 20 min. Cook: 1h Ready in: 1h 20 min. Servings: 4

Ingredients:

2 pounds pork spareribs
¼ cup honey
2 tbsp. soy sauce
2 tbsp. distilled white vinegar
1 clove minced garlic.
1 tbsp. brown sugar
½ tsp. baking soda
½ tsp. garlic salt

Cooking Directions:

Start by preheating the oven to 375 degrees F (190 degrees C)
Cut the ribs into separate pieces. Use a bowl to combine the honey, soy sauce, vinegar, garlic and brown sugar. Whisk until the honey and sugar is dissolved, then whisk in the baking soda. The baking soda will make the mix foam. Put the ribs in the bowl and coat them. Transfer the ribs to a sheet pan with aluminum foil. Glaze the ribs with excess sauce and sprinkle with garlic salt.
Bake for 1 hour, flipping them every 15 min.

Enjoy

11. Oven-Baked Kiwi-Lime Pork Ribs

Prep: 10 min. Cook: 1h Ready in: 1h 10 min. Servings: 6

Ingredients:

2 kiwis, peeled and sliced
½ cup white sugar
2 tbsp. cider vinegar
2 tbsp. lime juice
2 tbsp. salt
2 tbsp. chili powder
2 tbsp. cornstarch
1 clove minced garlic
3 pound country-style pork ribs

Cooking Directions:

Start by preheating the oven to 400 degrees F (200 degrees C). Put kiwis, sugar, vinegar, lime juice, salt, chili powder, cornstarch and garlic in a blender and blend until thickened into a sauce. Put the pork ribs on a sheet pan. Coat the ribs in the blended kiwi sauce and gently cover the ribs with a sheet of aluminum foil. Cook in the preheated oven for about 1 hour or until tender.

Enjoy

12. Grilled Cranberry Glazed Pork Ribs

Prep: 30 min. Cook: 1h Ready in: 1h 30 min. Servings: 6

Ingredients:

8 oz. whole cranberry sauce
1 cinnamon stick
1 tbsp. Dijon-style mustard
1 tsp. grated orange zest
1 ½ pounds country style pork ribs

Cooking Directions:

Start by firing up the grill.
Now take a saucepan and mix cranberry sauce, cinnamon stick, mustard and orange zest over medium heat for 5 minutes.
Place the ribs with a drip pan on the preheated coals at medium heat. Brush the ribs with sauce. Cover the grill and grill for 45 – 60 min. Keep brushing the ribs occasionally with sauce, until the ribs are tender.
Heat up the remaining sauce and serve with the ribs.

Enjoy

13. Oven-Baked Chinese Spareribs

Prep: 15 min. Cook: 1h 30 min Ready in: 1h 45 min. Servings: 6

Ingredients:

6 pounds pork spareribs
¾ cup Kikkoman Soy Sauce
½ cup honey
½ cup dry sherry
1 ½ gloves crushed garlic
¼ tsp. ground ginger

Cooking Directions:

Cut ribs into individual pieces and place them meaty side down on a sheet pan lined with aluminum foil.

Take a bowl and mix together Kikkoman Soy Sauce, honey, sherry, garlic and ginger. Brush the ribs with the sauce, but keep some for later

Cover the ribs with aluminum foil and bake at 350 degrees F (175 degrees C) for 1 hour.

Flip the ribs over and pour the remaining sauce over them. Bake them uncovered for another 30 min while brushing occasionally.

*_Enjoy_*

14. Grilled St. Louis-style Spareribs

Prep: 10 min. Cook: 3h 30 min Ready in: 4h 40 min. Servings: 4

Ingredients:

¼ cup dark brown sugar
3 tbsp. paprika
1 tbsp. dry mustard
1 tbsp. sea salt
1 ½ tsp. granulated garlic powder
1 ½ tsp onion powder
½ tsp. ground coriander
2 racks Extra Tender St. Louis Pork Spareribs
Vegetable oil
¾ cup apple juice

Cooking Directions:

Start of by taking a bowl and mix sugar, paprika, mustard, salt, garlic, onion powder and coriander. Coat both sides of ribs with a bit of vegetable oil and rub in the seasoning. Set the ribs aside for 1 hour at room temperature.

Start up the grill setting it up for indirect cooking at 230 – 250 degrees F (110 – 120 degrees C).

Place the ribs, meaty side down, over a drip and cook for 2 hours. Brush both sides with apple juice. Add about 10 charcoal pieces to the grill every 45 min. approx. to maintain the heat.

Remove the ribs from the grill and wrap each rack in aluminum foil. Put the ribs back on the grill and let them cook for 1 ½ to 3 hours until they are very tender. Again, add more coal as needed to maintain the temperature, if you're using a charcoal grill.

Unwrap the ribs and separate into individual pieces or serve as is.

Enjoy

15. Grilled Coconut Spareribs

Prep: 40 min. Cook: 1h 10 min Ready in: 9h 50 min. Servings: 4

Ingredients:

3 pounds pork spareribs
1 cup honey
½ cup coconut milk
1/3 cup lime juice
1 tsp. grated lime zest
3 cloves minced garlic
2 tbsp. minced fresh ginger root
2 chopped red chili peppers
4 chopped green onions
½ tsp. salt

Cooking Directions:

Start by placing the ribs in a saucepan and cover them with water. Bring them to a boil over high heat and, then let them simmer at medium heat for 40 min.

Remove the water and allow the ribs to cool to room temperature. Now take a bowl and mix together the honey, coconut milk, lime juice, lime zest, garlic, ginger, chili pepper, green onions and salt. Once thoroughly mixed add the ribs to the marinade and cover them up. Throw them in the refrigerator and let them sit overnight – occasionally turn the ribs to ensure full coverage of marinade.

Preheat the oven to 350 degrees F (175 degrees C).

Discard the marinade and put the ribs on a sheet pan.

Let them cook until fork tender, approx. 35 – 40 min.

Enjoy

16. Oven-Baked Cherry Short Ribs

Prep: 15 min. Cook: 4h 30 min Ready in: 4h 45 min. Servings: 6

Ingredients:

3 pounds beef short ribs
To taste salt
To taste pepper
4 tbsp. olive oil
1 chopped onion
2 stalks chopped celery
2 chopped carrots
1 bulb sliced fennel
1 cup Burgundy wine
3 sprigs fresh rosemary
8 sprigs fresh thyme
3 bay leaves
2 ½ tbsp. beef demi-glace
4 cups chicken stock
1 cup cherry cola
½ cup balsamic vinegar
2 cups pitted tart cherries
1 tbsp. butter

Cooking Directions:

Start by preheating the oven to 350 degrees F (175 degrees C).
Rub the short ribs with salt and pepper. Take an oven-ready pot and heat it over medium heat, until it is hot. Pour in about 2 tbsp. olive oil. Brown the ribs in the oil until golden brown on all sides.
Transfer the ribs to a plate and discard the oil.
Add another 2 tbsp. of olive oil to the pot and cook the onion, celery, carrots and fennel. Let it cook until the vegetables are soft and the onions translucent, approx. 8 min.
Pour in the Burgundy wine and bring it to a boil and let it cook until the mix is reduced to about half, approx. 10 min. Add the rosemary, thyme, bay leaves and demi-glace. Stir it well.
Mix in the chicken stock, cherry cola and balsamic vinegar.
Take the ribs and add them to the mix and cover them, so they are halfway covered. Baste the ribs in the liquid, bring the ribs to a boil over medium heat and cover.
Place the pot in the oven and let it cook until the meat lets go of the bone or approx. 3 ½ to 4 hours.

Enjoy

17. Oven-Baked Plum Glazed Pork Ribs

Prep: 55 min. Cook: 1h Ready in: 1h 55 min. Servings: 4

Ingredients:

3 pounds baby back pork ribs
1 cup chili sauce
7 oz. plum sauce
2 ½ tbsp. soy sauce

Cooking Directions:

Start by preheating the oven to 350 degrees F (175 degrees C).
Take a sheet pan and cover it with aluminum foil. Spray the foil with non-stick cooking spray.
Place the ribs on the foil and cook them uncovered for approx. 45 min.
Take a pot and mix the chili sauce, plum sauce and soy sauce and bring it to boil. Stir without pause.
When the ribs are done cooking, brush them with some of the sauce and put them back in the oven. Let them bake for approx. 45 – 60 min. until tender. Occasionally brush the rips while they are baking, about 4-5 times.

Enjoy

18. Grilled Raspberry Chipotle Back Ribs

Prep: 10 min. Cook: 3h Ready in: 4h 10 min. Servings: 4

Ingredients:

2 racks Pork Back Ribs

Dry rub
¼ cup light brown sugar
3 tbsp. sea salt
4 ½ tsp. chili powder
4 ½ tsp. dried lemon peel
4 ½ tsp. paprika
4 ½ tsp onion powder
2 tsp. cayenne pepper
2 tsp. black pepper

Sauce
1 cup seedless raspberry jam
¼ cup chipotle salsa
¼ cup white sugar
1 tsp. apple cider vinegar
¼ tsp. liquid smoke
¼ tsp. cayenne pepper

Cooking Directions:

Start by making the dry rub. Take a bowl and mix the brown sugar, salt, chili powder, dried lemon peel, paprika, onion powder, cayenne pepper, black pepper. Coat both sides of the ribs with the ribs and let them sit at room temperature for 1 hour.

Now start making the sauce. Take a saucepan and mix the raspberry jam, chipotle salsa, white sugar, apple cider vinegar, liquid smoke and cayenne pepper. Bring it to a boil over medium heat and let it simmer for 15 min. until it is thickened. Stir well. Let it cool and refrigerate it for later.

Start up the grill, either charcoal or gas for indirect cooking at 250 to 300 degrees F (120 – 150 degrees C).

To maintain the heat in a charcoal grill add about 10 coals every 45 min. approx.

Place the ribs, meaty side up, over a drip pan and grill them for 3-4 hours until very tender.

Move the ribs to direct heat and brush with the sauce. Let the sauce set, turn the ribs and brush the other side. Apply another layer to both sides.

Serve with remaining sauce.

Enjoy

19. Oven-Baked Hoisin Ribs

Prep: 15 min. Cook: 8h 30 min. Ready in: 8h 45 min. Servings: 6

Ingredients:

3 pounds pork ribs
1 tsp. salt
1 tsp. pepper
1 cup hoisin sauce
1 cup white sugar
½ cup white wine
2 tbsp. tomato paste
4 cloves crushed garlic
2 tsp. Asian chili-garlic sauce
½ tsp. Chinese five-spice powder

Cooking Directions:

Start by preheating oven to 350 degrees F (175 degrees C).
Spread the pork ribs on a sheet pan and season them with salt and pepper.
Bake in the preheated oven until golden brown, approx. 30 min.
Take a bowl and mix the hoisin sauce, sugar, soy sauce, white win, tomato paste, garlic, chili-garlic sauce and five-spice powder together in a bowl.
Transfer the ribs to the slow cooker insert and cover them with the hoisin sauce mixture.
Cook the ribs on Low until they are tender, approx. 8 hours.

Enjoy

20. Oven-Baked Cabernet Beef Short Ribs

Prep: 10 min. Cook: 2h 10 min. Ready in: 2h 20 min. Servings: 6

Ingredients:

2 pounds beef short ribs
2 tbsp. salt
2 tsp. garlic powder
2 tsp. ground black pepper
½ cup flour
2 tbsp. vegetable oil
4 cloves minced garlic
3 cups beef broth
1 cup Cabernet Sauvignon wine
1 sliced onion

Cooking Directions:

Start by preheating the oven to 350 degrees F (175 degrees C). Then move on to seasoning the ribs with salt, garlic powder and black pepper and rubbing flour on both sides of the ribs.

Heat oil in an oven-ready pot over medium-high heat. Cook about half the garlic in the oil until lightly browned, approx. 2 – 3 min. Add the short ribs and cook until completely browned, about 2 – 3 min. per side.

Pour beef broth and wine into the pot. Bring it to a boil and then add the rest of the garlic and sliced onion. Transfer the pot to the oven and let it bake for 2 hours.

Remove the ribs from the pot and put them on a plate. Bring the remaining liquid in the pot to a boil and cook until reduced in volume by half, approx. 5 – 7 min.

Coat the ribs with the sauce and serve.

Enjoy

21. Grilled Tennessee Style Back Ribs

Prep: 10 min. Cook: 4h Ready in: 4h 40 min. Servings: 4

Ingredients:

¼ cup brown sugar
¼ kosher salt
2 tsp. chili powder
1 ½ dry mustard
1 tsp. black pepper
1 tsp. celery salt
2 racks Extra Tender Pork Back Ribs
¼ cup yellow mustard
Apple juice

Cooking Directions:

Start by firing up either the charcoal or gas grill for indirect cooking at 250 degrees F (120 degrees C).
Now take a bowl and mix the sugar, salt, chili powder, dry mustard, pepper and celery salt.
Rub both sides of the ribs with yellow mustard and season with the dry rub.
Let them sit at room temperature for 30 min.
Place the ribs, meaty side up, over a drip pan and cook for 4 – 6 hours until tender. Occasionally spray apple juice over the ribs, every 30 min. or so.
Add 10 coals to a charcoal grill every 45 min. to maintain the heat.
Let the ribs stand 10 – 15 min. before serving.

*_Enjoy_*

22. Oven-Baked Asian Back Ribs

Prep: 10 min. Cook: 2h 10 min. Ready in: 4h 20 min. Servings: 4

Ingredients:

2 racks Pork Baby Back Ribs, cut into 3 – 4 rib sections
2 cups hoisin sauce
¼ cup rice wine vinegar
4 cloves minced garlic
3 tbsp. minced fresh ginger
1 tbsp. red chili flakes
2 tsp. brown sugar
3 tbsp. chopped green onions

Cooking Directions:

Start by taking a bowl and mix together hoisin sauce, rice wine vinegar, garlic, ginger, red chili flakes and sugar. Put the ribs in a resealable plastic bag and pour about ¾ marinade over the ribs. Seal the bag and refrigerate for 2 hours or over the night. The longer the ribs can marinade, the better.

Heat the oven to 325 degrees F (160 degrees C). Remove the ribs from the marinade and place them on a sheet pan with a piece of aluminum foil. Pour some of the marinade over the ribs and fold the aluminum foil over the ribs and seal.

Place the rib cooking pouch in the oven and cook until the ribs are tender, approx. 2 hours.

Turn up the oven to 450 degrees F (230 degrees C). Open the cooking pouch and remove the sauce and place the ribs back in the oven meaty side up. Roast them until they are browned and glazed. Coat the ribs with the rest of the marinade and drizzle green onions over them.

Enjoy

23. Grilled Sticky Molasses Spareribs

Prep: 10 min. Cook: 3h 10 min. Ready in: 4h 20 min. Servings: 4

Ingredients:

2 racks Extra Tender Pork Spareribs
Dry Rub
¼ cup light brown sugar
4 tsp. garlic powder
1 tbsp. chili powder
2 tsp. kosher salt
2 tsp. black pepper

Sauce:
½ cup honey
½ cup light molasses
½ cup balsamic vinegar
2 tbsp. canola oil
2 tbsp. whole grain Dijon mustard
2 tsp. black pepper
2 tsp. orange zest

Cooking Directions:

Start by making the dry rub about 1 hour before grilling. Take a bowl and mix together the brown sugar, garlic powder, chili powder, kosher salt and black pepper. Coat the ribs with the dry rub and let the ribs sit at room temperature for 1 hour.

Next make the sauce. Take a saucepan and mix together the honey, molasses, balsamic vinegar, canola oil, Dijon mustard, pepper and orange zest. Bring it to a boil over medium-high heat reduce the heat to medium and let it simmer for 10 min. until thickened. Stir well. Let it cool to room temperature, cover and refrigerate.

Fire up the grill, gas or charcoal, for indirect heat cooking at 250 – 300 degrees F (120 – 150 C).

Place the ribs with the meaty side up over a drip pan and let them cook for 4 hours until very tender.

Add 10 coals to a charcoal grill every 45 min. to maintain the heat. Place the ribs over direct heat and brush with the sauce. Let them cook for 5 min. until the sauce has set, then turn them around and brush the other side. Do this one more time.

Serve the ribs with the remaining sauce.

Enjoy

24. Grilled Peach Glazed Ribs

Prep: 5 min. Cook: 3h 40 min. Ready in: 3h 45 min. Servings: 4

Ingredients:

2 racks Extra Tender Pork Spareribs
1 cup peach jam
¼ cup chili sauce
2 tbsp. white vinegar
2 tbsp. water
1 tbsp. Worcestershire sauce
1 tsp. dry mustard
½ tsp. chipotle hot sauce
¼ tsp. onion powder
¼ tsp. garlic powder

Cooking Directions:

Start by firing up the grill, gas or charcoal, at 230 – 250 degrees F (110 – 120 C).
Place the ribs with the meaty side down over a drip pan. Let them cook for 2 hours.
Add 10 coals to a charcoal grill every 45 min. to maintain the heat.
Remove the ribs from the grill and wrap each rack in aluminum foil.
Put the wrapped ribs back on the grill and cook for 1 ½ - 2 hours more over indirect heat, until the ribs are very tender.
While the ribs are grilling make the glaze.
Take a small saucepan and mix together the peach jam, chili sauce, white vinegar, water, Worcestershire sauce, dry mustard, chipotle hot sauce, onion powder and garlic powder. Bring the mix to a boil over medium heat. Let it simmer for 30 min. Stir well.
Remove the ribs from the grill and unwrap. Place the ribs over direct heat and brush with the newly made peach glaze. Cook the ribs for 5 min. until the glaze is set. Turn the ribs over and brush the other side as well. Repeat this one more time.
After the second coating put the ribs on a plate and serve.

Enjoy

25. Grilled Kansas Barbecued Spareribs

Prep: 10 min. Cook: 4h 30 min. Ready in: 5h 40 min. Servings: 4

Ingredients:

2 racks Extra Tender Pork Spareribs
Dry rub
½ kosher salt
3 tbsp. light brown sugar
3 tbsp. white sugar
3 tbsp. black pepper
2 tbsp. chili powder
4 tsp. garlic powder
2 tsp. cayenne pepper
Sauce
½ cup apple cider vinegar
½ cup white vinegar
2 tbsp. light brown sugar
2 tbsp. hot sauce
2 tsp. cayenne pepper
2 tsp. kosher salt
1 tsp. black pepper

Cooking Directions:

Start by making the dry rub. Take a bowl and mix together the salt, sugar, black pepper, chili powder, garlic powder and cayenne pepper. Coat both sides of the ribs with the dry rub and let them sit at room temperature for 1 hour.

Meanwhile take another bowl and mix together the sauce. Whisk together the apple cider vinegar, sugar, hot sauce, cayenne pepper, kosher salt and black pepper.

Fire up the grill, charcoal or gas, for indirect cooking at 250 degrees F (120 degrees C).

Add 10 coals to a charcoal grill every 45 min to maintain the heat. Place the ribs with the meaty side up over a drip pan. Let them cook for 4 ½ to 5 ½ hours until very tender. Baste the rips with the sauce every hour.

Serve the ribs with remaining sauce.

Enjoy

26. Grilled Missouri Style St. Louis Ribs

Prep: 10 min. Cook: 3h 40 min. Ready in: 4h 50 min. Servings: 4

Ingredients:

2 racks Extra Tender Pork Spareribs
Vegetable oil

¼ cup barbecue rub

Sauce

18 oz. bottle ketchup
1 cup honey
1 cup white vinegar
¼ cup water
¼ cup light molasses
1 tbsp. chili seasoning blend
2 tsp. liquid smoke
1 tsp. dry mustard
½ tsp ground allspice

Cooking Directions:

Start by coating both sides of the ribs with vegetable oil and season them with the barbecue seasoning. Let them sit at room temperature for 1 hour.

Fire up the grill, gas or coal, for indirect cooking at 230 – 250 degrees F (110 – 120 degrees C).

Place the ribs with the meaty side down over a drip pan. Let them cook for 2 hours.

Add 10 coals to a charcoal grill every 45 min. to maintain the heat. Remove the ribs from the grill and wrap them in aluminium foil. Put the wrapped ribs back on the grill and cook for another 1 ½ - 3 hours over indirect heat, until the ribs are very tender.

While the ribs are grilling in the foil make the sauce. Take a saucepan and mix together the ketchup, honey, white vinegar, water, light molasses, chili seasoning blend, liquid smoke, dry mustard and ground allspice.

Bring it to a boil over medium heat and let it simmer for 15 minutes. Stir well.

Remove the ribs from the grill, unwrap them and put them back on direct heat on the grill. Brush them with the newly made sauce. Cook for 5 min. until the sauce is set. Turn the ribs and brush the other side. Do this one more time and serve.

Enjoy

27. Grilled Cider Spareribs

Prep: 15 min. Cook: 6h 10 min. Ready in: 7h 25 min. Servings: 6

Ingredients:

2 racks Extra Tender Pork Spareribs
3 tbsp. chili powder
2 tbsp. kosher salt
5 tsp. granulated garlic powder
5 tsp. black pepper
½ cup apple cider vinegar
½ cup water
¾ cup barbecue sauce

Cooking Directions:

Start by making the dry rub. Take a bowl and mix together the chili powder, salt, garlic powder and pepper. Keep ½ cup of the dry rub for later. Rub the rest of it on both sides of the ribs. Let them sit at room temperature for 1 hour.

Take a new bowl and add vinegar, water and the ½ dry rub.

Fire up the grill, gas or charcoal, for indirect heat at 250 degrees – 300 degrees F (120 – 150 degrees C). Place the ribs with the meaty side down on a drip pan. Let them grill for 5 ½ to 6 ½ hours.

Add 10 coals every 45 min. to maintain the correct temperature. Brush the rips with barbecue sauce and cook them for another 5 min. until the sauce sets. Brush the other side and let it set for 5 min. Repeat once more and serve.

Enjoy

28. Grilled Lemon Pepper Pork Back Ribs

Prep: 10 min. Cook: 3h 30 min. Ready in: 4h 40 min. Servings: 4

Ingredients:

2 racks Extra Tender Pork Back Ribs
Vegetable oil
3 tbsp. sea salt
1 tbsp. ground white pepper
1 tbsp. onion powder
2 tsp. cayenne pepper
1 ½ tsp. dried lemon peel
½ tsp. ground apple pie spice

Cooking Directions:

Start by making the dry rub. Take a bowl and mix together the sugar, salt, white pepper, onion powder, cayenne pepper, lemon peel and apple juice spice.
Coat both sides of the ribs with vegetable oil and rub in the dry rub. Let the ribs sit at room temperature for 1 hour.
Fire up the grill, gas or charcoal, for indirect heat at 230 degrees – 250 degrees F (110 – 120 degrees C). Place the ribs with the meaty side down on a drip pan. Let them grill for 2 hours.
Add 10 coals every 45 min. to maintain the correct temperature.
Wrap the ribs in aluminium foil and return them to grill for another 1 ½ to 2 hours until they are tender.

Enjoy

29. Oven-Baked Hawaiian Spareribs

Prep: 15 min. Cook: 2h Ready in: 2h 15 min. Servings: 6

Ingredients:

3 pounds pork spareribs, cut into bit size pieces
¼ cup vinegar
½ cup ketchup
1 tbsp. soy sauce
8 oz. can crushed pineapples
3 tbsp. brown sugar
2 tbsp. cornstarch
½ tsp. salt
½ tbsp. fresh ginger

Cooking Directions:

Start by preheating the oven to 325 degrees F (165 degrees C).

Take a saucepan and whisk together the vinegar, ketchup, soy sauce and pineapple and place it over medium heat. Add the brown sugar, cornstarch, salt and ginger. Stir constantly until thickened, approx. 5 min.
Layer the spareribs in a roasting pan. Pour half of the sauce over the top of them and add another layer on top, topping off with the remaining sauce. Cover with aluminium foil and bake in a preheated oven until done, approx. 1 ½ - 2 hours.

Enjoy

30. Sesame and Root Beer Glazed Ribs

Prep: 20 min. Cook: 2h 30 min. Ready In: 14h 50 min. Servings: 8

Ingredients:

3 tbsp. Asian sesame oil
3 tbsp. chili-garlic sauce
1 tsp. salt
2 racks lamb ribs
1 (12 oz.) bottle root beer
2 tsp. salt or to taste
2 tsp. ground black pepper or to taste
3 gloves garlic
¼ cup chopped green onions
¼ cup rice vinegar
1 tbsp. Asian chili pepper sauce
2 tsp. toasted sesame seeds

Cooking Directions:

Start by pouring sesame oil, chili-garlic sauce, and 1 tsp. salt in a mixing bowl and mix together. Place the ribs onto a piece of aluminium foil and brush the mixture onto both sides of the ribs. Place ribs into a resealable plastic bag and pour the root beer over the ribs and seal the bag. Refrigerate 12 hours minimum, or during the night. Remove ribs from marinade and save the marinade in a refrigerated state for later use.

Preheat the oven to 250 degrees F (120 degrees C). and place a piece of aluminium foil onto a sheet pan. Place the rib racks with the meat-side up, onto the foil and season both sides with salt and black pepper. Place a piece of parchment paper on top of the meat and then another piece of aluminium foil over the parchment paper. Fold the edges to create an airtight seal making a cooking pouch.

Bake the ribs in the preheated oven for about 2 hours or until fork-tender. Open the cooking pouch to test.

Transfer the refrigerated marinade to a pot. Add garlic, green onions and rice vinegar to the marinade and bring it to a boil. Reduce the heat and cook and stir until sauce is reduced by half (approx. 5 min.). Pour juices from cooking pouch into the pot with the sauce and add Asian chili pepper sauce.

Bring back to a simmer and cook the sauce until lightly thickened to a glaze (approx. 5 min.). Increase oven temp. to 450 degrees F (230 degrees C). and line another sheet pan with foil and transfer the ribs to sheet pan. Brush both sides of ribs with the glazing sauce. Cook in the oven until glaze begins to cook onto meat (6 – 7 min.). Brush another coat of glaze onto the ribs and repeat 4 times, increasing cooking 5 – 6 minutes per time until meat is glazed and fully fork tender.

Brush one more coat of glaze onto the meat and sprinkle the glaze with sesame seeds. Cook for 5 more minutes to set the last glaze coat.

Enjoy

Thank you for purchasing
Top 30 Most Delicious Ribs Recipes.

We hope you found the recipes as tasteful and delicious as we do.

Please show your support and love for ribs by leaving a review on Amazon.

Printed in Great Britain
by Amazon